7 FACTS

NO PAPER CORE MANUFACTURER TELLS YOU

FIRST AND ONLY BOOK WRITTEN.... ON PAPER CORE INDUSTRY

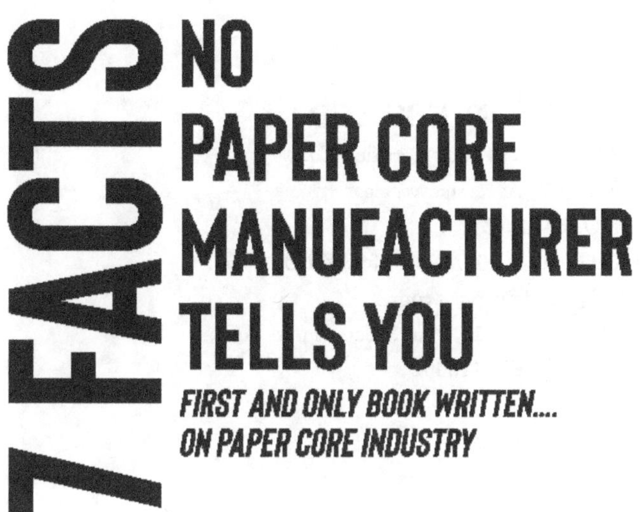

HIMANSHU CHATURVEDI

Worldwide Published by
Pendown Press

PENDOWN PRESS LLP

An ISO 9001 & ISO 14001 Certified Co.,

Regd. Office: 3767A, Kanhaiya Nagar,

Tri Nagar, Delhi-110035

Ph.: 8130886000, 9650072927, 8595249536

E-mail: info@pendownpress.com

Branch Office: 1A/2A, 20, Hari Sadan, Ansari Road,

Daryaganj, New Delhi-110002

Ph.: 011-45794768

Website: PendownPress.com

First Edition: 2024

ISBN: 978-93-5554-889-4

Layout and Cover Designed by Pendown Graphics Team
Printed and Bound in India by Thomson Press India Ltd.

CONTENTS

GRATITUDE

Dear Grandparents,

As I sit down to pen these words, my heart swells with gratitude for the immense impact you both have had on my life. However, today I want to shine a spotlight on someone who has been not just a grandfather but a guiding light, a mentor, and a source of inspiration – Shri Kanhiya Lal Sharma, my dearest grandfather.

Dada ji, your presence in my life has been nothing short of a blessing. Your unwavering commitment to your principles, your tireless dedication to family, and your boundless love have shaped me in ways I can't even begin to express. Your values, etched in every word you speak and every action you take, have become the blueprint for the person I am today.

Your teachings have been my compass, guiding me through life's ups and downs with grace and resilience. Your wisdom, shared through countless stories and quiet conversations, has illuminated my path even in the darkest of times. And your love, so pure and unconditional, has been my rock, grounding me amidst life's storms.

Dada ji, you are not just my grandfather; you are my hero, my role model, and my pillar of strength. I am endlessly grateful for the lessons you've taught me, the love you've bestowed upon me, and the person you've helped me become.

With all my love and deepest respect,

Himanshu Chaturvedi

INTRODUCTION

I'm Himanshu Chaturvedi, the Manufacturing & Marketing Director at Rashmi Paper Products, India's leading paper core manufacturer, with 15 years of industry experience.

As a second-generation entrepreneur, I've been passionately dedicated to revolutionizing manufacturing and packaging since joining my family business in 2009. My mission is to tackle every packaging challenge facing the Indian paper core industry, driving innovation and excellence every step of the way.

Excited for the journey ahead as we continue reshaping the future of packaging at Rashmi Paper Products. It is the solution finding approach and desire to innovate and offer world class product that led me to create our unique selling proposition (USP) -the Innovation, Technology, and Excellence(I.T.E) framework.

The I.T.E framework harnesses cutting-edge technology and continuous innovation in manufacturing processes to produce paper cores that offer superior performance, efficiency, and sustainability. We prioritize exceptional service with a focus on responsiveness, communication, and support throughout the entire ordering and manufacturing process, thus fostering long-term relationships with clients.

My 15-year professional journey stands as a testament to relentless dedication, continuous experimentation, and invaluable experience. Together with my team, we have been instrumental in assisting multinational and Indian paper core companies, consistently delivering precision and quality within record time frames.

Motivated by a deep commitment to serving our clients and customers, I have channelled my extensive knowledge and insights into the Indian paper core industry into, *'7 Facts NO PAPER CORE MANUFACTURER TELLS YOU.'* This book, set for public release in March2024, is a must-read for all paper core manufacturing brands.

Within its pages, you'll discover how to overcome everyday challenges and craft superior, cost-effective paper cores tailored for various industries, including textiles, paper mills, and the yarn industry. Packed with a handy checklist and the ultimate paper core troubleshooting guide, this book is essential reading for anyone seeking to excel in the realm of paper core manufacturing.

❖   ❖   ❖   ❖

ACKNOWLEDGEMENTS

I am deeply thankful to the wonderful individuals who have played a crucial role in making this book a reality and guiding me through this journey to its completion:

- ➤ To my cherished family, whose steadfast support and unwavering belief have been the cornerstone of my endeavours. To my dear parents and my grandfather whose boundless love and guidance have sculpted the person I am today.

- ➤ A heartfelt appreciation to my brother, whose constant encouragement and inspiration have been a source of strength.

- ➤ My beloved wife, Anjali, has been my rock and source of love throughout this transformative journey.

- ➤ To my daughters, Janisha and Prisha, your resilience and positivity continuously propel me forward, motivating me to make a meaningful impact.

- ➤ A profound debt of gratitude to my mentor, Akshar Yadav sir, whose invaluable wisdom and guidance have illuminated my entrepreneurial path.

- ➤ To the dedicated team at Rashmi Paper Products,I am deeply thankful for your commitment and tireless efforts,which have played a pivotal role in the significant success of our collective mission.

> Finally, I express sincere appreciation to our esteemed customers, vendors, partners, and well-wishers. Your solid belief in our vision and unconditional backing have been integral to our journey.

> I am thankful to my friend Dinesh Verma, CEO, Pendown Press and his team for their support and suggestions throughout the creative process.

THANK YOU ALL FOR YOUR EVERLASTING BELIEF AND SUPPORT.

MY STORY

Hello, my name is Himanshu Chaturvedi, and I hail from the beautiful state of Uttar Pradesh.

It all began about ten years ago when I started working as a paper core marketer. Right from the start, I was fascinated by how useful paper cores could be in building strong relationships with clients and bringing in leads for my business. Since then, paper core has been a key part of my marketing strategy, consistently giving me tangible results.

My family background has played a big role in shaping my career path. My grandfather, Shri Kanhiya Lal Sharma, taught me the importance of hard work and perseverance. My father, Shri Subhash Chaturvedi, worked as a production manager in a steel company, and from him, I learned the value of dedication and entrepreneurship.

In 1988, my father took a loan from friends and relatives to start his own business, initially in socks manufacturing. Later, in 1999, he moved into the paper core and paper tube industry, starting with trading in used paper cores and tubes. Growing up, I remember listening to my father's conversations with clients, which sparked my interest in the business world.

Following my passion, I joined the family business after completing my twelfth exams in 2009. Alongside that, I pursued a B. Tech degree in computer science, graduating in July 2013. In 2014, we shifted from trading to manufacturing, which was a significant milestone for us.

Over the years, I've kept upgrading my skills and techniques to grow our business. Along the way, I've been fortunate to help many small business owners, startups, large companies, and entrepreneurs improve their paper core selections for success.

My grandfather always used to say, "tu jis field me haath dalega usi field me tarraki karega logon ko new disha dikhayega or apna or apne parivar ka naam roshan karega" (Whatever field you venture into, you will excel in that field, show people a new direction, and illuminate the name of yourself and your family).

Believe me, you have the potential to succeed!
Himanshu Chaturvedi

THANK YOU!

To each and every reader who has joined me on this remarkable journey, I extend my heartfelt gratitude for choosing **'7 Facts NO PAPER CORE MANUFACTURER TELLS YOU'** as your guide. Your decision to be a part of this endeavour is deeply appreciated, and I am truly thankful for your trust.

It is my sincere hope that the insights shared within these pages will ignite a spark of inspiration within you. May they empower you to conquer obstacles, pursue your aspirations with unwavering determination, and ultimately, achieve greatness beyond imagination.

Once again, thank you for your trust and for embarking on this journey with me. Together, let us dare to dream and strive for the extraordinary.

WHY THIS BOOK?

You might be wondering why I'm sharing this story instead of charging for it. The reason is simple: I believe in sharing knowledge to empower others. By using the insights in this story, you can also achieve remarkable growth and success in your business. Furthermore, I have three reasons of sharing this masterpiece with you:

1. First, being in love with paper core, it breaks my heart to see how people abuse it. So, I want to put as many people as possible on the right path.

2. Second, People often say the paper core industry is messy and disorganized. Because I've had a good education, I want to change that. I want to make things more organized and efficient. And not just for myself – I want to help everyone in the industry do better. When the industry is well-organized, everyone can succeed and grow their businesses. So, by organizing things, I hope we can all do well together.

3. Third, I am unable to coach everyone personally due to time constraints, so this book is my gift to business owners, large companies, purchasing managers, production managers, general managers, and startups. It shares 7 valuable lessons that I have learned during my journey as a creative paper core manufacturer.

I hope these lessons will steer you towards success with the right choice of paper core.

So, without further ado, let's explore 7 Lessons I Learned About Paper Core...

Your Friendly Paper Core Expert,
Himanshu Chaturvedi

EXPLORING PAPER DYNAMICS: ESSENTIALS FOR PAPER CORE MANUFACTURING

Paper products play an essential role in our daily lives, serving various applications and packaging needs worldwide. However, environmental factors, particularly humidity and moisture, can significantly affect the performance and appearance of paper tubes and cores.

In regions experiencing all four seasons, the fluctuating climate poses unique challenges. High humidity levels during summer can lead to heightened temperatures, while dry, cold winters can exacerbate conditions. These environmental variations not only impact individuals but also affect fibrous paper products.

Understanding how paper interacts with its surroundings is really important to make sure these products stay strong and work well.

DRY CONDITION

➤ In dry environments, paper products can release moisture, especially during winter months, leading to quicker shrinking or warping of paper tubes and cores. Keep in mind that paper is made of tiny fibers held together by hydrogen bonds, and it always absorbs some moisture. As air temperature decreases, its moisture-retaining capacity diminishes.

➢ Several factors affect shrinkage in dry conditions, including wall thickness, paper width, and tube weight. Generally, winding products experience about 0.006 inches per inch of shrinkage, while recut products have around 0.003 inches per inch.

➢ When it's really cold and you've got the heating on indoors, the air gets even drier. This can cause the same kinds of problems you might feel at home—dry air, stuffy noses, and static electricity. And just like at home, this dry air can make paper cores shrink because the moisture evaporates.

HUMIDITY

➢ As temperatures rise, the air's capacity to hold moisture increases, leading to quicker absorption of moisture by paper fibers. Consequently, paper tubes and cores tend to expand in high-humidity environments.

➢ Regions with frequent rainfall, experiencing high humidity during summer months, are particularly susceptible to these effects. In such conditions, paper cores manufactured in high humidity (e.g., 90% R.H.) can undergo significant shrinkage if placed in air-conditioned rooms with low humidity levels.

➤ During the manufacturing process, paper tubes typically start with 12% moisture content, drying to 8% with silicate glue and 8.5-9% with P.V.A. glue, resulting in less shrinkage and warping when P.V.A. glue is used.

➤ Packaging methods also play a role. Cores stored flat on pallets, bundled, or on racks may experience greater effects from humidity and temperature changes, leading to inconsistencies among cores. Stretch-wrapping during shipment can increase moisture levels unless promptly removed upon receipt.

STORAGE

➤ Proper storage of paper tubes and cores is critical, especially when it comes to humidity and moisture. To keep them at the right size, it's best to them in ideal conditions, ideally at 73°F and 50% relative humidity (R.H.). Relative humidity indicates the amount of water present in the air at a specific temperature, expressed as a percentage of the maximum water capacity at that temperature.

TUBE DIMENSIONAL STABILITY

➤ Since paper have HYGROSCOPIC PROPERTY, it expands or contracts as it absorbs or releases moisture. The stability of paper tubes' dimensions, including their inside and outside diameters, wall thickness, and length, is greatly influenced by fluctuations in moisture content. Paper isn't consistent in how it changes size either; it might change in length, width, weight, or thickness in different ways because it's anisotropic.

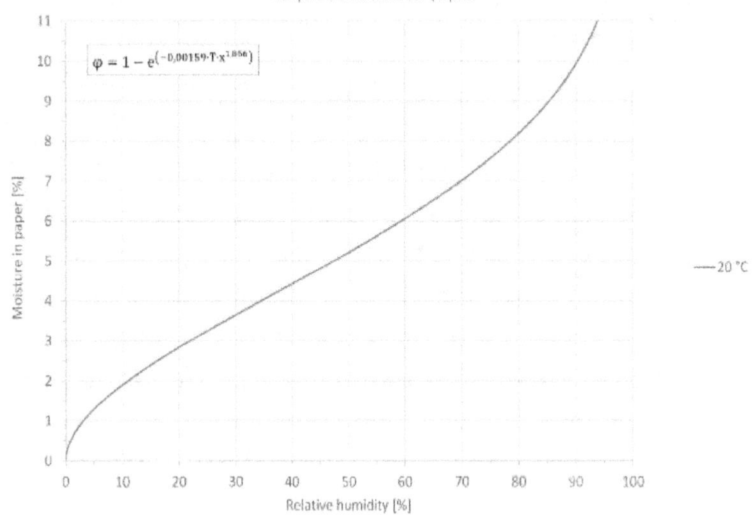

$$\varphi = 1 - e^{\left(-0{,}00159 \cdot T \cdot x^{1.856}\right)}$$

> ➤ High humidity can weaken paper tubes and cores, making them more likely to fail. To reduce the effects of moisture, it's best to use paper products as soon as you get them.

> ➤ ***If products arrive stretch-wrapped, it's advisable to remove the wrapping immediately, as changes may occur once unwrapped.*** Also, try not to store paper tubes and cores near heaters, air conditioners, or places where air is being humidified or dehumidified. Where you store them matters too; make sure they're kept somewhere they won't get squashed or bent.

SUMMARIZATION

> As evident from the discussion, grasping the impact of moisture and humidity on paper tubes and cores is crucial for end-users seeking optimal appearance and performance. Keeping the relative humidity (R.H.) and temperature just right in where you make and store them ensures they work great. When you're ordering paper tubes and cores, it's important to know what sizes you need for length (L), inner diameter (I.D.), outer diameter (O.D.), thickness (T), and weight (W). At **Rashmi Paper Products,** all our products are tailor-made to meet your exact specifications.

STRENGTH MATTERS

*(Exploring the Link between Paper Tube
Stability and Product Quality)*

The quality of the product is directly linked to the strength of the core. If the core's strength is insufficient, it will result in product damage.

Case Study

On a previous occasion, a client of mine (whose name I can't reveal due to confidentiality) opted for tubes from a different vendor at a marginally lower rate. Although the tubes were cheaper, upon usage during production, they proved brittle and collapsed when materials were wound onto them.

Despite securing the tube at a marginal 20 paisa discount, they made a compromise on the price, inadvertently leading to significant losses. Let's delve deeper into the magnitude of their loss: Their yarn, priced at ₹350 per kg, typically winds around 2 to 2.5 kg onto each tube. Considering a 2 kg winding, the loss amounts to 350 * 2 = ₹700, while for a 2.5 kg winding, it totals 350 * 2.5 = ₹875. Thus, the party faced a loss ranging from ₹700 to ₹875, solely due to the seemingly insignificant 20 paisa discrepancy in the purchase price.

That's why I'm emphasizing the importance of not comparing tubes based on a slight variance of 10-20 paisa and refraining from assuming that we're saving ₹875. Had my client not been focused on the 20 paisa difference, they could have potentially saved a considerable amount, surpassing ₹875. This shift in perspective would have transformed today's losses into profits.

The quality of a product is closely tied to the strength of its paper core, particularly evident in industries like textiles and yarn where paper tubes play a crucial role.

In the textile industry, paper tubes serve as essential components for winding yarn during manufacturing processes. A strong paper core ensures the stability and integrity of the yarn package. If the paper core lacks sufficient strength, it may deform or collapse under the tension exerted by the wound yarn, leading to irregularities in the final product. Additionally, weak paper cores can result in difficulties during handling, transportation, and storage, potentially causing damage to the yarn and compromising its quality.

Similarly, in the yarn industry, paper tubes are indispensable for packaging and transporting yarn products. A durable paper core is essential for maintaining the shape and structure of the yarn package, preventing deformations, tangling, or breakages during handling and transit. Moreover, the quality of the paper core directly influences the overall durability and stability of the yarn package, ensuring that the yarn remains intact and protected throughout the supply chain.

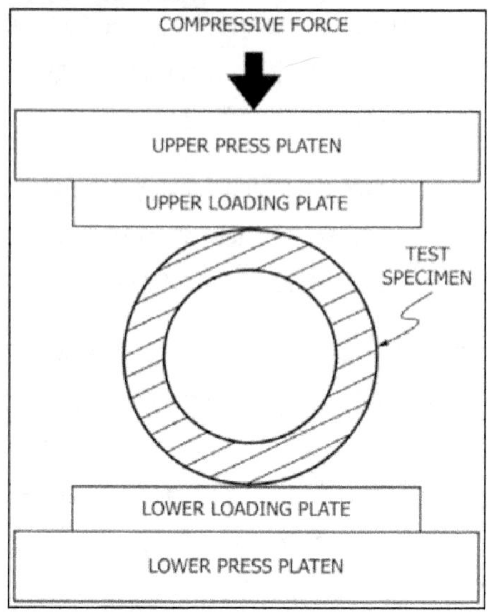

Therefore, the strength of the paper core is paramount in ensuring the quality, stability, and reliability of products,especially in industries such as textiles and yarn. A robust paper core not only enhances the performance and efficiency of manufacturing processes but also safeguards the integrity of the final product, ultimately contributing to customer satisfaction and brand reputation

The strength of a paper core is typically measured using various testing methods designed to assess its mechanical properties and performance under different conditions. Some common methods for measuring the strength of a paper core include:

1. **Burst Strength Test:** This test determines the resistance of the paper core to bursting under pressure. It involves applying hydraulic pressure to the core until it bursts, with the pressure at which the burst occurs being recorded as the burst strength.

2. **Crush Test:** In this test, the paper core is subjected to compressive force to assess its ability to withstand crushing. The core is placed between two plates, and pressure is applied until the core deforms or collapses. The force required to cause deformation is measured as the crush strength.

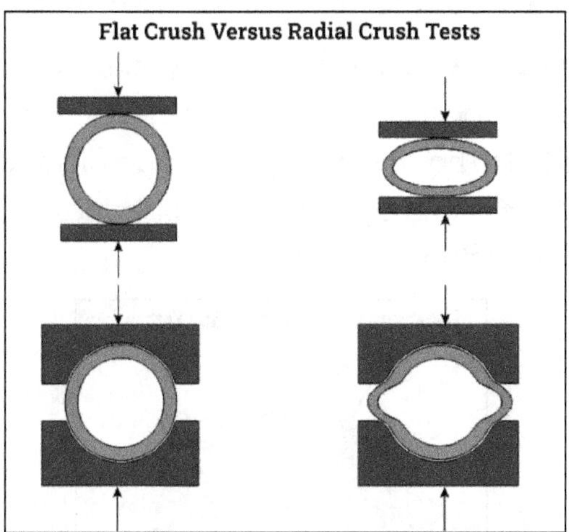

3. **Tensile Strength Test:** This test evaluates the ability of the paper core to resist pulling or stretching forces. It involves applying tensile force to the core in opposite directions until it breaks. The maximum force sustained by the core before failure is recorded as the tensile strength.

4. **Edge Crush Test (ECT):** This test assesses the resistance of the paper core to edge compression. It involves applying pressure to the edges of the core to measure its ability to withstand crushing along the edges.

These testing methods provide valuable insights into the strength and durability of paper cores, helping manufacturers ensure that their products meet quality standards and performance requirements.

So, if the strength of the paper tube is low, it can have several negative implications for the quality of the product:

➢ **Structural Integrity:** A weak paper tube may not be able to support the weight or tension of the product it is intended to hold. This can lead to deformities, collapse, or breakage of the product during handling, storage, or transportation.

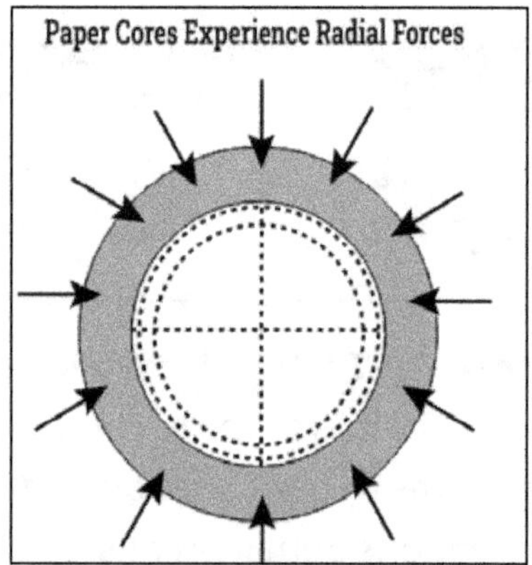

> **Stability:** A low-strength paper tube may lack stability, causing the product to wobble, tilt, or shift within the tube. This instability can result in damage to the product or compromise its appearance.

> **Protection:** Paper tubes are often used to protect products from external elements such as moisture, dust, or impact. A weak paper tube may fail to provide adequate protection, leaving the product vulnerable to damage or contamination.

> **Handling and Transport:** Weak paper tubes can pose challenges during handling and transportation, increasing the risk of mishaps such as tearing, bending, or crushing. This can lead to product loss, rejection, or customer dissatisfaction.

> **Overall Perception:** The quality of packaging reflects on the perceived quality of the product itself. A flimsy or poorly constructed paper tube may give the impression of inferior quality, affecting consumer confidence and brand reputation.

In summary, a low-strength paper tube can compromise the structural integrity, stability, protection, handling, and overall perception of the product, ultimately impacting its quality and marketability. Therefore, it's essential to ensure that paper tubes used for packaging are of sufficient strength to meet the requirements of the product they contain.

OUTER DIAMETER OPTIMIZATION

(Maximizing Core Performance and Quality)

If the outer diameter (O.D) of your core is not correct, during the rewinding process, some rolls maybe wound tightly while others maybe wound loosely on the slitting machine or any other rewinding machine.

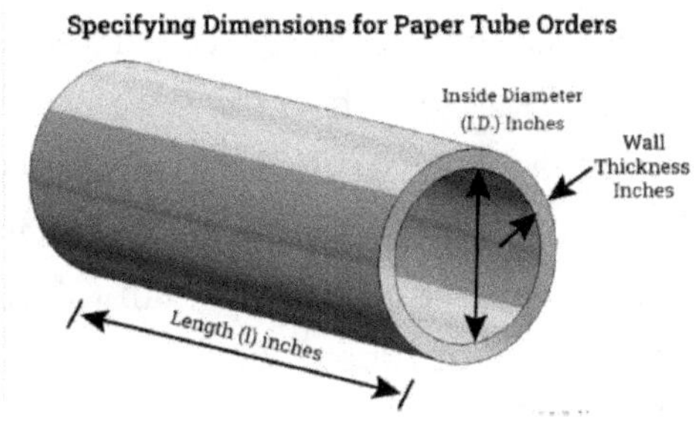

Paper exhibits hygroscopic properties, meaning it absorbs or releases moisture from the surrounding environment, causing fluctuations in its dimensions. Consequently, the outer diameter of the core can vary from season to season.

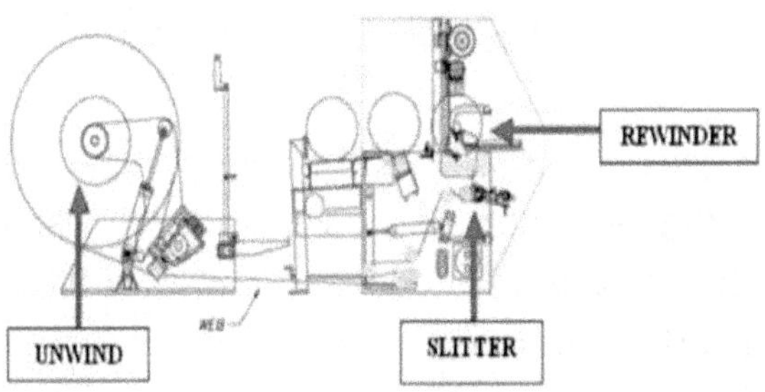

When rolls are rewound too loosely due to inconsistent core diameter, the material may scatter, leading to inefficiencies and wastage. This scattering might require extra packaging material to secure the material properly. Moreover, if the material scatters excessively, it may become unusable, resulting in significant losses of valuable resources.

Ensuring a well-defined outer diameter of paper cores is crucial for delivering a quality product for several reasons:

> **Consistent Winding:** A uniform outer diameter ensures consistent winding of materials such as paper, film, or fabric. When the core's outer diameter is consistent, each layer of material is wound evenly, preventing uneven tension and wrinkles. This consistency is essential for maintaining product integrity and appearance.

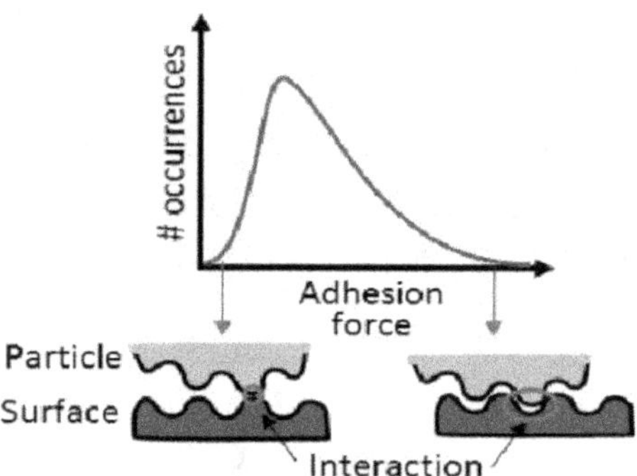

Example: In the production of adhesive tapes, if the outer diameter of the core varies, it can lead to uneven winding of the tape. This can cause problems during application, such as uneven adhesion or difficulty in dispensing the tape smoothly.

➢ **Compatibility with Machinery:** Machinery used for winding or unwinding materials is typically designed to accommodate specific core sizes. Well-defined outer diameters ensure compatibility with such machinery, minimizing the risk of jams, misfeeds, or other operational issues.

Example: In a printing press, if the outer diameter of the paper core is not well-defined, it may not fit properly onto the mandrel. This can result in misalignment during printing, leading to print defects or machine downtime.

➢ **Product Protection:** Properly sized cores provide structural support and protection to the material wound around them. A clearly defined outer diameter prevents excessive movement or shifting of the wound material, thereby reducing the risk of damage during handling, transportation, or storage.

Example: In the textile industry, fabric rolls are often wound onto paper cores for storage and transportation. If the outer diameter of the core is inconsistent, it may fail to provide adequate support to the fabric, leading to creases, tears, or other forms of damage.

➢ **Efficient Material Usage:** Well-defined outer diameters optimize material usage by minimizing waste. When cores maintain consistent dimensions, manufacturers can accurately calculate the amount of material needed for each roll, reducing excess material and associated costs.

Example: In the packaging industry, where materials like plastic film are wound onto cores, a precise outer diameter ensures that each roll contains the intended amount of material. This prevents overuse of film and reduces material waste.

In conclusion, maintaining a well-defined outer diameter for paper cores is essential for ensuring consistent winding, compatibility with machinery, product protection, and efficient material usage. These factors collectively contribute to delivering a quality product to customers.

LAMINATION INTEGRITY AND TUBE STABILITY

(How Poor Lamination Compromises Paper Tube Integrity)

Based on my experience, when paper lacks proper lamination or isn't adequately adhered to the tube, it tends to peel off. Subsequently, if the paper detaches from the tube, particularly when the tube is spinning at high revolutions per minute (RPM), there's a risk that it may strike the paper operator. This is especially concerning given that the machine typically operates at speeds of around 1500 to 1800 RPM. Moreover, insufficient lamination can lead to the collapse of the tube itself. Therefore, it underscores the importance of ensuring proper lamination for the integrity and safety of the manufacturing process.

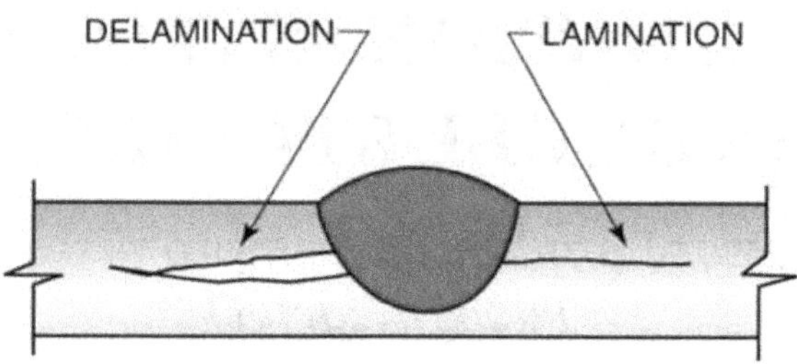

Now let us understand how poor lamination poses a significant threat to the integrity of paper tubes due to several key factors:

1. **Weak Bonding:** Inadequate lamination results in a weak bond between the paper layers and the tube surface. This weak bond fails to provide the necessary structural support to hold the layers together, making the tube prone to unravelling or separation.

2. **Increased Vulnerability to Moisture:** Poorly laminated paper tubes are more susceptible to moisture penetration. Moisture can seep through gaps or imperfections in the lamination, leading to swelling or warping of the paper layers. This compromises the structural integrity of the tube, making it prone to deformation or collapse.

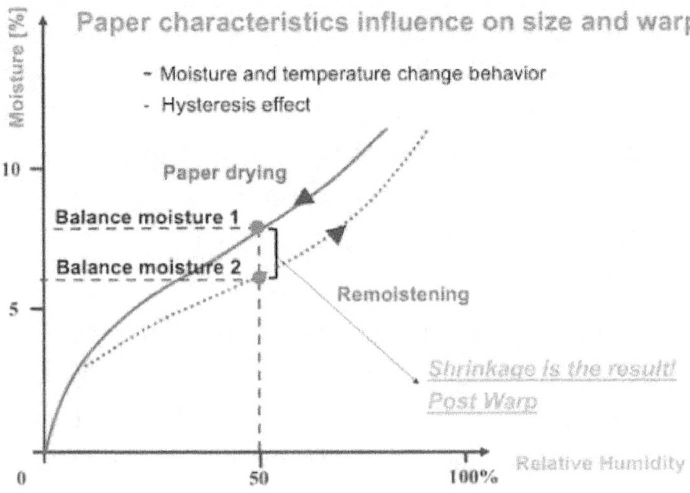

3. **Reduced Strength and Stability:** Proper lamination reinforces the strength and stability of paper tubes by effectively bonding the layers together. In contrast, poor lamination results in uneven bonding or delamination, weakening the structural integrity of the tube. This compromises its ability to withstand external forces, such as pressure or impact, increasing the risk of damage or failure.

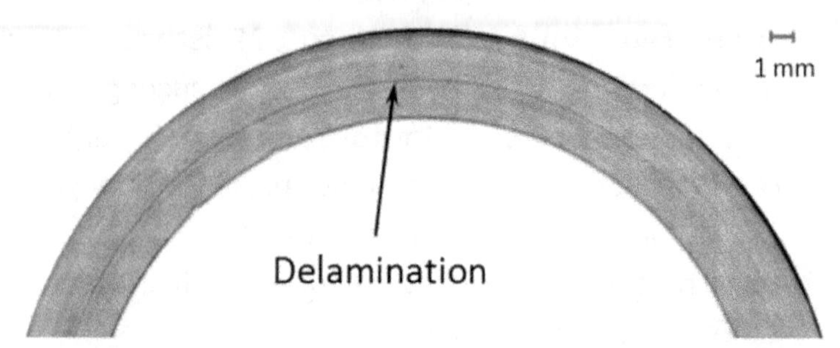

4. **Risk of Unraveling:** Inadequate lamination fails to securely anchor the paper layers to the tube's surface. As a result, the layers may begin to peel or unravel over time, especially during handling, transportation, or storage. This not only compromises the appearance of the tube but also undermines its functionality and performance.

5. **Potential for Production Disruptions:** Poorly laminated paper tubes may lead to production disruptions due to frequent stoppages for rework or repairs. These interruptions not only impact productivity but also incur lead to costs and delays in fulfilling orders.

In conclusion, poor lamination compromises the integrity of paper tubes by weakening their structural strength, increasing vulnerability to moisture, and raising the risk of unraveling. Addressing lamination issues is crucial to ensure the reliability, performance, and longevity of paper tube products.

Now I'll tell you the methods of enhancing the bonding strength and overall integrity of the tubes:

1. **Selection of High-Quality Adhesive:** Choosing a high-quality adhesive that is specifically formulated for paper-to-paper bonding is essential. The adhesive should provide strong adhesion and ensure proper bonding between the layers of paper and the tube surface.

2. **Optimization of Lamination Process:** Proper control and optimization of the lamination process are crucial for achieving consistent and uniform bonding. This includes controlling factors such as adhesive application rate, temperature, pressure, and drying time to ensure optimal bonding strength and adhesion.

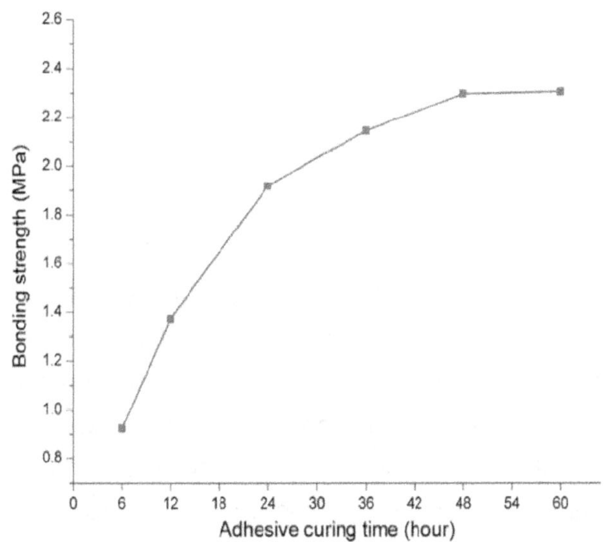

3. **Surface Preparation:** Ensuring that the surface of the paper tube is clean, dry, and free from contaminants is essential for promoting proper adhesion. Any residues or contaminants on the surface can interfere with the bonding process and compromise lamination quality.

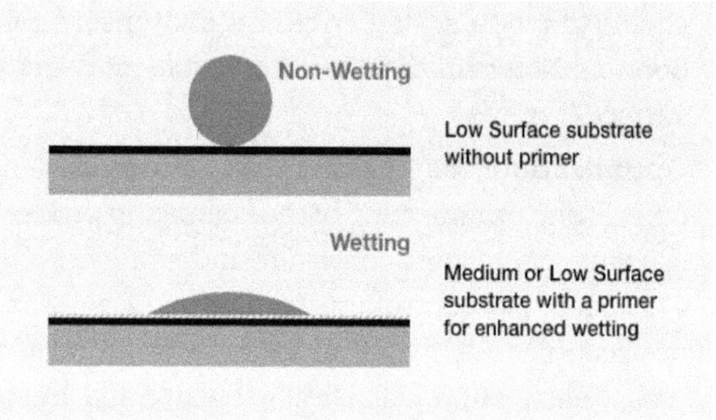

4. **Quality Control Measures:** It's crucial to have strict quality control measures in place throughout the lamination process to spot and fix any defects or issues early on. This may include visual inspection, adhesive testing, and performance testing to ensure that the lamination meets required standards.

5. **Training and Skill Development:** Providing training and skill development opportunities for personnel involved in the lamination process can help improve techniques and practices. Proper training ensures that operators understand the importance of lamination quality and follow the best practices to get the best results.

6. **Investment in Equipment and Technology:** Investing in modern lamination equipment and technology can improve efficiency, accuracy, and consistency in the lamination process. Advanced equipment may offer features such as precise adhesive application, automated controls, and real-time monitoring to ensure quality and reliability.

7. **Feedback and Continuous Improvement:** Setting up a feedback system and carrying out continuous improvement efforts are vital for pinpointing areas that need improvement and making necessary corrections. Gathering feedback from stakeholders and incorporating lessons learned into the lamination process fosters a culture of continuous improvement and quality excellence.

By implementing these measures, manufacturers can significantly improve lamination quality in paper tubes, resulting in stronger, more durable, and more reliable products that meet customer expectations and industry standards.

To enhance lamination in paper tubes, key steps include selecting high-quality adhesive, fine-tuning the lamination process parameters, ensuring surface cleanliness, implementing rigorous quality control measures, providing training for personnel, investing in modern equipment, and fostering a culture of continuous improvement. These measures collectively improve bonding strength, consistency, and overall product integrity, resulting in stronger, more reliable paper tubes that meet quality standards and customer expectations.

INNER DIAMETER EXCELLENCE

(Maximizing Core Performance through Precision)

The inner diameter (I.D.) of a paper tube refers to the measurement of the diameter of the hollow space inside the tube. It is basically the size of the central opening or bore of the tube where materials such as paper, film, fabric, or other products are wound or stored. The inner diameter is very important for how well the paper tube works and how it performs, affecting different parts of its production, handling, and use.

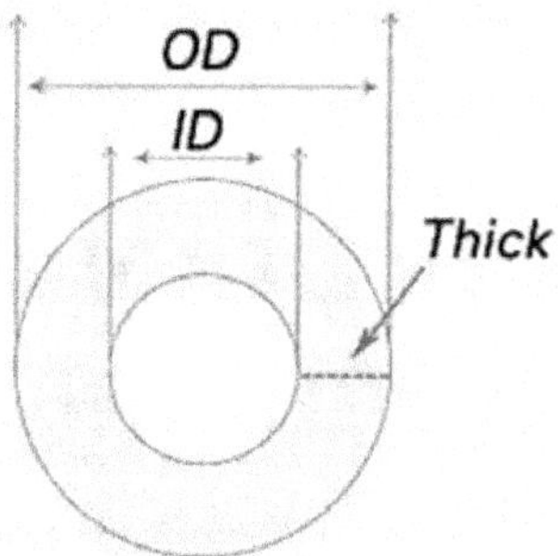

Thickness=(OD-ID)/2

Overall, the inner diameter of a paper tube is a critical parameter that directly impacts its functionality, performance, and suitability for various applications. Properly defining and maintaining the inner diameter is essential for ensuring the quality, reliability, and effectiveness of paper tubes in diverse industrial and commercial settings. We at Rashmi Paper Products customizes the paper tube according to the requirements (like I.D, O.D, length, paper quality, etc.) of our clients.

Now, let us understand why a well-defined inner diameter (I.D) is crucial for the production of perfect tubes:

1. **Consistency in Material Winding:** A properly sized inner diameter ensures uniform winding of materials such as paper, film, or fabric around the core. When the I.D. is consistent, each layer of material is wrapped evenly, preventing uneven tension and wrinkles in the final product.

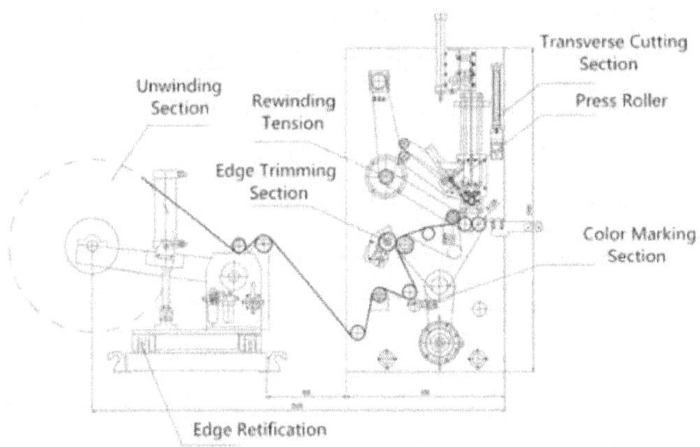

Example: In the manufacturing of adhesive tapes, if the inner diameter of the core is inconsistent, it can lead to uneven winding of the tape. This may result in variations in adhesive coverage, affecting the tape's performance and appearance.

2. **Compatibility with Machinery:** Industrial machinery used for winding or unwinding materials is typically designed to fit specific core sizes. Having

a well-defined inner diameter ensures that the core is compatible with such machinery, minimizing the risk of jams, or other operational issues.

Example: In a slitting machine used for cutting materials into narrower widths, if the inner diameter of the core varies, it may not fit properly onto the mandrel. This can result in misalignment during cutting, leading to irregular or damaged edges on the material.

3. **Structural Integrity of the Tube:** A properly sized inner diameter provides structural support to the tube, ensuring its stability and preventing deformation or collapse during handling, transportation, or storage.

Example: In the textile industry, fabric rolls wound onto cores with inadequate inner diameter may lack sufficient support. This can result in sagging or collapsing of the rolls, leading to damage to the fabric and making handling more difficult.

4. **Prevention of Collapse on Machinery:** If the inner diameter of the tube is not proper, it can lead to collapse or deformation of the tube when subjected to high-speed processing on machinery such as slitting machines.

Example: During the slitting process, if the inner diameter of the core is too large or too small, it may not provide adequate support to the material being slit.

This can cause the tube to collapse or deform under the pressure exerted by the slitting blades, resulting in production stoppages and material waste.

So, I suggest a well-defined inner diameter is essential for the production of perfect tubes as it ensures consistency in material winding, compatibility with machinery, structural integrity of the tube, and prevention of collapse or deformation during processing. Failure to maintain proper inner diameter can lead to various production issues and compromise the quality of the final product.

Now, let's understand the various losses and inefficiencies that can arise if the inner diameter (I.D.) of a paper tube is not correct:

1. **Material Wastage:** Improper inner diameter may result in overuse or under use of materials during winding or storage. Overuse occurs when the I.D. is too large, requiring more filler material consumption than necessary. Conversely, under use happens when the I.D. is too small, causing leftover material that cannot be wound onto the tube effectively.

2. **Production Delays:** Incompatible inner diameters can cause production delays due to issues such as machinery jams, or stoppages. If the I.D. does not match the specifications of the winding or processing equipment, it can lead to interruptions in production, requiring adjustments or repairs to the machinery.

3. **Quality Issues:** Incorrect inner diameter may result in quality issues such as uneven winding, wrinkles, or creases in the wound material. These defects can compromise the appearance, performance, or functionality of the final product, leading to customer dissatisfaction or rejection of the goods.

4. **Operational Costs:** Inefficient use of materials, production delays, and quality issues associated with improper inner diameter contribute to increased operational costs. This includes expenses related to material wastage, downtime for machinery maintenance or repairs, and rework to rectify quality defects.

5. **Logistical Challenges:** Inconsistent inner diameter can pose logistical challenges during transportation, storage, or handling of the paper tubes and their contents. Tubes with varying inner diameters may not stack or fit together efficiently, leading to inefficiencies in logistics operations and increased space requirements.

6. **Customer Impact:** Ultimately, the losses associated with improper inner diameter can impact customer satisfaction and trust in the supplier's ability to deliver quality products reliably and consistently. Quality issues or delays caused by incorrect inner diameter may lead to lost sales, customer complaints, or damage to the supplier's reputation.

Therefore, ensuring the proper inner diameter is essential for minimizing losses and optimizing the efficiency and effectiveness of paper tube production processes.

NOTE: Paper's hygroscopic property (discussed earlier in chapter 1) may cause slight alterations in the inner diameter (I.D.).

Lesson - 5

LENGTH PRECISION

(Ensuring Paper Core Length Consistency)

The length of a paper core refers to the measurement of the core's longitudinal dimension, typically from one end to the other. This dimension is really important in various industries where paper cores are used, such as packaging, textiles, printing, and converting.

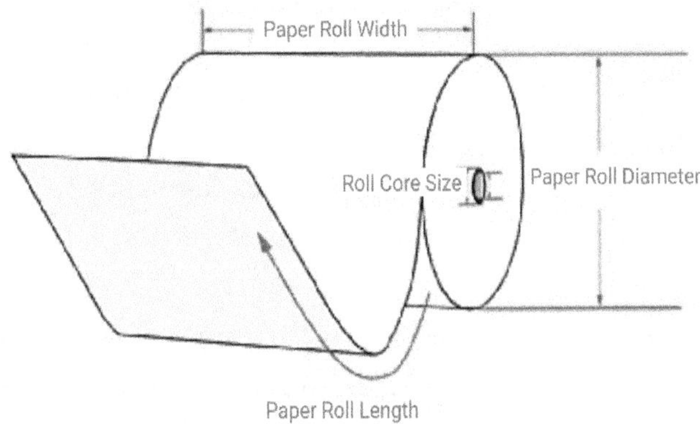

The length of a paper core is a crucial factor in ensuring the production of the right product for several reasons:

1. **Compatibility with Material:** The length of the paper core must be appropriate for the material it will hold or wind. If the core is too short, it may not accommodate the entire length of the material, leading to inefficiencies, waste, or the need for additional handling. Conversely, if the core is too long, excess material may be required to fill the space, resulting in unnecessary costs and material usage.

2. **Optimal Winding:** The length of the paper core influences the efficiency and effectiveness of the winding process. A properly sized core ensures that the material is wound evenly and securely, without gaps or overlaps. This promotes uniformity in the final product and prevents issues such as uneven tension, wrinkles, or bulges.

3. **Equipment Compatibility:** The length of the paper core must be compatible with the specifications of the winding or processing equipment used in manufacturing. If the core is too long, it may not fit properly onto the equipment's mandrel or spindle, leading to operational issues such as jams, or damage to the equipment.

4. **Product Performance:** The length of the paper core can impact the performance and functionality of the final product. For example, in industries such as textiles or printing, the length of the core may affect the ease of handling, transportation, or installation of the wound material. An improperly sized core may result in difficulties during product use or may not meet customer expectations.

5. **Cost Efficiency:** Selecting the right length for the paper core can contribute to cost efficiency in manufacturing processes. By optimizing core length, manufacturers can minimize material waste, reduce production downtime, and streamline handling and storage processes. This helps maximize resource utilization and improve overall profitability.

6. **Customer Satisfaction:** Ultimately, the length of the paper core can impact customer satisfaction and the perception of product quality. A properly sized core ensures that the material is wound neatly and securely, leading to a professional appearance and positive user experience. Consistently, Rashmi Paper Products Team keeps in mind to deliver products with the right core length that reinforces customer trust and loyalty.

Properly sizing the core length contributes to the overall effectiveness, efficiency, and success of manufacturing processes.

Now, let us understand what happens if the length of a paper tube is not properly defined, it can lead to several issues and potential losses, including:

➢ **Bubbling and Delamination:** In addition to length-related issues, improper sizing of paper tubes can also lead to bubbling and delamination. Bubbling occurs when air becomes trapped between layers of material during winding, resulting in bubbles or pockets beneath the surface.

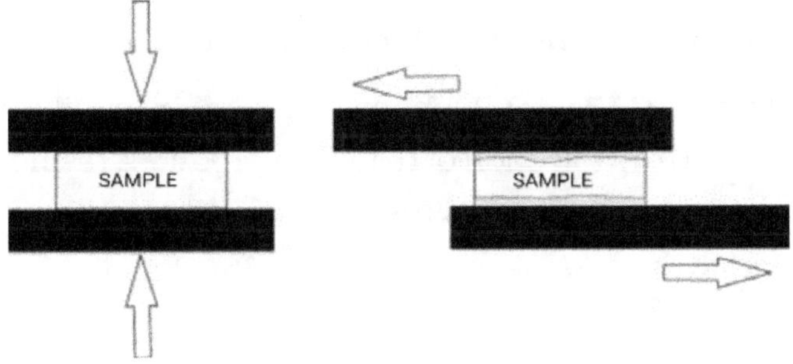

Delamination occurs when the layers of material separate from each other due to inadequate bonding. Both bubbling and delamination can compromise the structural integrity and appearance of the wound material.

Delamination occurs when the layers of material separate from each other due to inadequate bonding. Both bubbling and delamination can compromise the structural integrity and appearance of the wound material.

➢ **Auto drop failure:** In automated manufacturing processes, such as those involving conveyor systems or packaging machinery, auto drop failure can occur if the paper tubes are not of the correct length. If they're too long or too short, automated systems may not be able to handle them properly, leading to malfunctions or errors in the drop or release mechanisms. For instance, if a conveyor system is programmed to drop tubes into packaging containers of specific sizes, tubes of incorrect lengths may not fit properly, resulting in jams or blockages in the system.

Losses resulting from these issues can include:

1. **Material Waste:** Bubbling and auto drop failure can lead to the rejection of defective products, resulting in wasted materials and resources.

2. **Production Downtime:** Malfunctions in automated systems due to improper tube lengths can cause downtime in production, leading to delays in order fulfilment and potential loss of revenue.

3. **Rework and Scrap:** Defective products may need to be reworked or scrapped, costing extra money and resources to fix the problems.

4. **Damage to Equipment:** Jams or blockages caused by tubes of incorrect lengths can damage machinery and equipment, resulting in repair or replacement costs.

Overall, we at Rashmi Paper Products ensures proper definition of the length of paper tubes which is essential to avoid these losses and maintain efficiency and quality in manufacturing processes. It requires careful planning, accurate measurements, and adherence to quality control standards throughout the production process.

NOTE: *Due to hygroscopic property (as discussed in chapter 1) of paper, Length (L) of paper tube can vary slightly.*

BEARING THE LOAD

(The Significance of Paper Tube Weight)

In a manufacturing setup, there exists a specified tolerance limit, often expressed as a percentage, within which the weight of the paper tube must fall. If the actual weight goes beyond this limit, it can have big effects on the outer diameter (O.D.) of the tube, which we discussed in Chapter no.2.

When the weight exceeds the tolerance limit, the tube's outer diameter may increase, leading to challenges during the winding process. Excessive weight can cause the paper to stretch or expand, altering the dimensions of the tube. This change in outer diameter can disrupt the uniformity and stability of the winding process, resulting in difficulties in producing tightly wound rolls or causing uneven tension distribution across the material.

Conversely, if the weight of the tube falls below the specified tolerance limit, the outer diameter may decrease. This reduction in diameter can lead to insufficient support for the wound material during the winding process, potentially causing sagging or wrinkling of the material on the roll.

Additionally, variations in outer diameter can affect the performance and functionality of downstream processes, such as labeling, packaging, or handling of the finished rolls.

Example: "Let's consider a scenario where a yarn manufacturer is producing yarn packages, each weighing a total of 1000 grams. Typically, out of this total weight, 100 grams are attributed to the paper tube onto which the yarn is wound.

Now, if there is an increase in the weight of the paper tube, let's say by 50 grams, making it 150 grams in total, this means that only 850 grams of yarn can be wound onto the tube. In this case, the yarn manufacturer might face accusations of cheating from customers because they are receiving less yarn than expected for the same total weight. This can damage the reputation of the yarn manufacturer and lead to customer dissatisfaction.

Moreover, the increase in the weight of the paper tube results in losses for the paper tube manufacturer. They are now using more material to produce each tube without any additional benefit, which can significantly impact their profitability.

On the other hand, if the weight of the paper tube decreases, for example, by 20 grams, making it 80 grams in total, the yarn manufacturer now needs to wind 920 grams of yarn onto the tube to meet the total weight of 1000 grams per package.

This results in losses for the yarn manufacturer, as they are providing more yarn for the same total weight. Additionally, the decrease in the weight of the paper tube may affect its structural integrity and performance, leading to potential issues during handling and storage."

In summary, variations in the weight of paper tubes used for winding yarn can have significant consequences for both yarn manufacturers and paper tube manufacturers. It can lead to accusations of cheating, customer dissatisfaction, and financial losses for both parties involved.

To maintain the weight of the paper tube for a high-quality product, several factors need consideration:

1. **Consistency in Material:** Make sure to useconsistent sourcing of materials and quality control measures to keep the paper uniform throughout tube manufacturing. This consistency helps in achieving predictable weights for the tubes.

2. **Accurate Measurements:** Use precise weighing scales and measurement tools during the manufacturing process to ensure that each paper tube meets the specified weight requirements.

3. **Standardized Manufacturing Processes:** Establish standardized manufacturing processes that include precise cutting, shaping, and assembly techniques to consistently produce paper tubes of the desired weight.

4. **Quality Control Checks:** Implement regular quality control checks at various stages of production to identify and rectify any deviations in weight promptly. This may include visual inspections, weight measurements, and adherence to predefined tolerances.

5. **Moisture Control:** Monitor and control moisture levels in the paper material throughout the manufacturing process. Fluctuations in moisture content can affect the weight of the paper tubes, so it's essential to maintain consistency in this aspect.

6. **Machine Calibration:** Ensure that manufacturing machinery involved in the process, such as cutting and winding machines, are properly calibrated to produce paper tubes of the intended weight consistently.

7. **Customer Communication:** Communicate openly with customers about any potential variations in tube weight that may occur due to factors such as moisture content or machine settings. Transparency helps manage customer expectations and fosters trust.

8. **Continuous Improvement:** Continuously evaluate and improve manufacturing processes to optimize efficiency and minimize variations in tube weight. Regular reviews and feedback mechanisms can help identify areas for improvement and implement corrective actions.

By focusing on these aspects, paper tube manufacturers can effectively maintain the weight of their products, ensuring consistency, quality, and customer satisfaction.

At **Rashmi Paper Products,**we always make sure to maintain the weight and if there is any variation due to moisture **(Hygroscopic Property)** or machine differences, we communicate it clearly with the customer.

REFINING THE CORE

(Understanding Edge Polishing in Paper Tubes)

If the edges of the paper tube are not adequately polished, it can cause a bunch of problems during the unwinding process of yarn. Poorly polished edges may cause the yarn to snag or catch as it comes off the tube, disrupting the smooth flow of material. This interruption in the unwinding process can result in production delays and decreased efficiency at the customer's facility.

Furthermore, the quality of the yarn may be compromised due to the irregular unwinding caused by unpolished edges. The yarn may experience increased tension or friction, leading to stretching, breakage, or other defects. As a result, the customer may observe inconsistencies in the tensile strength and overall quality of the yarn, which can affect the performance of their end products.

On top of that, the appearance of unpolished or faulty edges on the paper core reflects negatively on the overall quality of the product. Customers may perceive such flaws as indications of poor craftsmanship or manufacturing standards, leading to dissatisfaction and loss of trust in the supplier.

The polishing of paper tubes is typically done using specialized machinery and techniques designed to smooth and refine the edges of the tubes. Here's a general

overview of the process:

1. **Preparation:** Before polishing, the paper tubes are usually cut to the desired length and formed into cylindrical shapes through a winding process. Any excess material or rough edges may be trimmed or removed to prepare the tubes for polishing.

2. **Polishing Machinery:** Various types of polishing equipment are available, including sanders, grinders, and buffing machines, each suited for different tube sizes and polishing requirements. These machines use abrasive materials or polishing compounds to make the tube edges smooth.

3. **Abrasive Materials:** Depending on the specific polishing needs, abrasive materials such as sandpaper, emery cloth, or polishing pads may be used. The choice of abrasive material depends on factors such as the type of paper used for the tubes and the desired level of smoothness.

4. **Polishing Process:** The paper tubes are fed into the polishing machine, where they undergo a series of polishing steps. The abrasive material is applied to the edges of the tubes, either manually or automatically, to remove any roughness or imperfections.

5. **Finishing Touches:** After the initial polishing, finer abrasive materials or polishing compounds may be applied to achieve a smoother finish and enhance the appearance of the edges. The tubes may undergo

multiple passes through the polishing machine to ensure uniformity and consistency in the polishing process.

6. **Quality Control:** Throughout the polishing process, quality control measures are implemented to inspect the tubes for any remaining imperfections or irregularities. Any tubes that do not meet the specified quality standards may be rejected or undergo further polishing.

7. **Packaging:** Once the polishing process is complete and the tubes have been inspected and approved, they are typically packaged and prepared for shipment to customers or further processing in downstream manufacturing operations.

Overall, the polishing of paper tubes involves careful attention to detail and the use of specialized equipment and techniques to achieve smooth, refined edges that meet the quality standards required for various applications.

Therefore, team of **Rashmi Paper Products** ensures proper edge polishing of paper cores that is essential not only for facilitating smooth unwinding and maintaining yarn quality but also for upholding the reputation and reliability of the manufacturer in the eyes of the customer. It underscores the importance of meticulous attention to detail and quality control measures throughout the paper core manufacturing process.

AUTO DOFFING FAILURE AND TUBE DYNAMICS

(Understanding Edge Polishing in Paper Tubes)

There are two types of automatic doffing methods used in ring-spinning machines: stationary and travelling devices, with the former being more common in newer machines. After a doff, the doffer, equipped to hold both empty and fully wound bobbins, rises from below. Fully wound cops are gripped by the doffer and transferred to it, while empty bobbins are moved from the doffer to the spindle of the ring-spinning machine. The doffer then returns to its initial position and transfers all full cops to a conveyor belt, often leading to the winding machine.

"Autodoff failure" refers to a malfunction in the automatic doffing system of spinning machines. It occurs when the system fails to remove full bobbins or packages of spun yarn and replace them with empty ones as intended. This can lead to production downtime and decreased productivity. Preventive measures include regular maintenance and operator training.

POY, FDY, DTY Tubes

- **Partially Oriented Yarn (Poy):**

  It is suitable for fine, coarser, as well as micro-denier polyester filament yarn.

- **Salient features:**
  - Dimensional stability for automated winders
  - Auto doffing efficiency over 99.5%
  - Smooth surface for complete unwinding of yarn
  - Excellent horizontal strength to sustain yarn tension and package weight
  - Excellent vertical strength to eliminate damage during transportation and auto handling
  - Excellent tail-end efficiency
  - Round edges for smooth unwinding
  - Bleed-free Parchment paper for easy identification
  - Recyclability

> ## Standard Product Range:

I	Min.	Max
ID	75 mm	125 mm
Thickness	3 mm	15 mm
Length	115 mm	282 mm
Weight	150 gms	490 gms
Moisture	8%	9%
Spinning Speed		4000 mpm
Yarn Tension	8 gms/denier	30 gms/denier
Denier Range	100	500
Radius ID	1R	2R
Radius OD	2R	3R
Notch/Slit	Customised notches for varying technologies and wide range of deniers	
Colour	Available in 60 plus range of VP/GP papers	
Winding Technologies	Suitable for Barmag, Dupont, Enka, Murata, Teijin, Toray, Unitika, Zimmer	

'Rashmi Paper Products' textile tubes are high in strength, performance, and dimensional stability. These tubes are manufactured in state of the art plants to ensure global benchmarked quality.

> **Fully Drawn Yarn (Fdy):**

Series for FDY Technology Winders

> **Applications:**

For the latest technology winders with speeds up to 7000 mpm for micro filament fully drawn yarn, Team Rashmi Paper Products offers a product that is tailor-made to provide quality and consistency to yarn manufacturers.

> **Salient features:**

- Dimensionally stable
- Ideally suitable for the latest automated winders
- Special top layer papers and adhesives to prevent tube bursting at start-up
- Extra hard tube to withstand yarn tension at 7000 mpm
- High vertical strength for damage-free transportation and storage
- 3 R Edge Polish for direct application on weaving
- Modern technology for consistent notch profile, depth, and location
- Low tolerance length for consistent location of notch at string up
- Bleed-free color parchment papers for easy identification

➤ **Standard Product Range:**

	Min.	**Max**
ID	94 mm	120 mm
Thickness	3.5 mm	15 mm
Length	115 mm	200 mm
Weight	215 gms	460 gms
Moisture	8%	9%
Spinning Speed		7000 mpm
Yarn Tension	8 gms/denier	30 gms/denier
Denier Range	50	100
Radius ID	1R	2R
Radius OD	2R	3R
Notch/Slit	Customised notches for varying technologies and wide range of deniers	
Colour	Available in 60 plus range of VP/GP papers	
Winding Technologies	Suitable for Barmag, Dupont, Enka, Murata, Teijin, Toray, Unitika, Zimmer	

'Rashmi Paper Products' textile tubes are high on strength, performance, and dimensional stability. These tubes are manufactured in state of the art plants to ensure global benchmarked quality.

- ➢ **Drawn Twisted Yarn (Dty):**

  Series for Quality DTY Tubes

- ➢ **Applications:**

  Our team excels in manufacturing products with consistent quality, offering maximum operational efficiency and a wide range of choices. Cost competitiveness to meet market dynamics is at the core of all developments at Rashmi Paper Products.

- ➢ **Salient features:**

  - Specially designed bull nose suitable for perfect end cap fittings

  - Straightness to avoid vibration during yarn winding

  - Smooth surface to eliminate layer falling

  - High strength to sustain pressure during extended doffing times

  - Ideally suited for speeds ranging from 800 mpm - 1100 mpm

  - "C" cut radius at straight end for Open-end cap fitting

  - High vertical strength for damage-free transportation and storage

  - Exceptionally good dimensional stability

  - Available in range and combinations of bleed-free VP/GP papers

➢ **Standard Product Range:**

	Min.	Max
ID Open End	51 mm	69 mm
ID Bull Nose End	42 mm	58 mm
Thickness	2 mm	6mm
Length	160 mm	290 mm
Weight	140 gms	220 gms
Moisture	8%	9%
Spinning Speed	800-1100 mpm	30 gms/denier
Denier Range	50 - 500	100
Radius ID	1R	2R
Radius OD	2R	3R
Notch/Slit	Customised notch for varying technologies and wide range of deniers	
Colour	Available in 80 plus range of GP/ VP papers	
Winding Technologies	Suitable for Barmag, Murata, RPR, Scrag, Teijin	

'Rashmi Paper Products' textile tubes are high on strength, performance and dimensional stability. These tubes are manufactured in state of the art plants to ensure global benchmarked quality.

Highlights:

- ➤ Customized window, notch, and groove designs tailored for optimal string-up efficiency.

- ➤ Superior dimensional stability ensured by our precise 100% length and 100% outside diameter measurement systems during tube manufacturing.

- ➤ Sleek surface finish and meticulously polished edges for seamless yarn unwinding.

- ➤ **Innovative Bull-nosed, POY and FDY Tubes:**
  - Specially engineered bull-nosed edge facilitates smooth yarn unwinding.
  - Elimination of plastic caps at yarn unwinding points.
  - Reduced yarn breakage, particularly beneficial for fine-denier yarns.
  - Enhanced productivity and minimized machine downtime.
  - Utilization of bobbins at full capacity, minimizing yarn wastage.
  - Improved edge durability for enhanced resistance during yarn package handling.

❖ ❖ ❖ ❖

RECAP

Let's take a moment to recap the key topics we've explored in these seven valuable chapters:

> Strength

> Poor lamination

> Inner Diameter (ID)

> Outer Diameter (OD)

> Length

> Weight

> Polishing

> Auto Doffing

CALL TO ACTION

Dear Readers,

As we reach the end of this book, I would like to express my deepest gratitude for taking the time to read this book. By this chapter, you might be thinking, "Himanshu, why and how have you shared everything so transparently?" My father always guided me to "share the valuable lessons for free."

So, what have I done? I have shared all that I have learned from years of experience, including setbacks and successes. Now, you have two choices:

1st choice:

I have provided you with all the information, and you can implement it yourself. However, as per my experience, you would face a lot of hurdles, and the cost you would pay for that would be huge.

Alternatively, you can move ahead with the 2nd choice:

2nd choice:

You can have me and my team by your side, making implementation easy and stress-free.

If you wish to proceed with the 2nd choice, you can schedule a one-on-one meeting with me.

Email ID: hims.napster@gmail.com

Contact Details: 9999706615

Warm Regards,

Himanshu Chaturvedi